Hackers and Cybersecurity

The Battle to Protect Digital Privacy

Table of Contents

Chapter 1. Introduction

In today's interconnected digital landscape, the battle to protect digital privacy is of paramount importance. Our Special Report on "Hackers and Cybersecurity: The Battle to Protect Digital Privacy" delves into this increasingly urgent concern in a language accessible to all, no matter your technical aptitude. From the clandestine world of hackers to the fortresses of cybersecurity, we'll guide you through the intricate maze these two perspectives weave. Whether you're a concerned internet user, a privacy advocate, or just an enthusiastic learner, join us in shedding light on the invisible war that impacts us all - safeguarding our precious digital privacy. This compelling narrative brings you to the frontline of information warfare, making the complex world of cybersecurity not just comprehensible but fascinating. Needless to say, understanding cybersecurity will level up your digital literacy, making this Special Report a wise investment today for a safer, more informed tomorrow.

Chapter 2. Introduction: The Digital Battlefield

In the silence of the virtual ether, a war is waged. This war is cryptic, evasive, and far from tangible yet perilously real. It threatens one of our most valued contemporary possessions: digital privacy. As we immerse ourselves into the depth of this narrative, we peel away the layers of a world that burrows deeper into servers and software, intruders and defenders, data and security - the world of hackers and cybersecurity.

Digital Warfare

2.1. The Invisibly Visible Threat

The internet, in its broadest sense, is a vast multi-dimensional universe. Ephemeral digitalised cities, connected by obscure electrical currents, house billions within their silicon walls. Every post we share, every purchase we make, every byte of data we produce, contributes to the ever-expanding digital metropolitan sprawl. In this unbounded landscape, every one of us is a citizen, leaving our unique digital footprint. But while the land appears serene and subdued, danger lurks at every corner, injected into the fabric of the internet by those with nefarious intentions.

The threats are not just theoretical; they are increasingly practical and real, impacting individuals and organisations alike. In 2020, reported cyber crimes resulted in over \$4.2 billion in losses in the U.S. alone, a damning testament to the severity of this invisible war. The number of data breaches per year has skyrocketed, threatening not only corporate markets but also affecting the most intimate facets of our lives - social security numbers, bank accounts, private conversations, healthcare records, and more - all existing in the vulnerable crossfire.

2.2. Age of Data: Stealthy Commodification

Data has become the most sought-after resource, denoted as the 'new oil.' Every second, quintillions of bytes are generated, creating mind-boggling conglomerates of information. Data can provide granular insights into demographics, behaviours, and interests, precious knowledge for entities looking to understand, predict, or manipulate patterns. On the darker side, this information can also be exploited, leading to misuse with potentially damaging consequences. This stealthy commodification of data has made it a high-value target for those seeking to hack, steal, and profiteer.

Among the noteworthy targets, let's take a look at Big Data databases. They're repositories of hefty quantities of structured and unstructured data. Storage services, social media channels, international corporations, each stockpile vast pools of data, making them prime targets for hackers. Due to the economic, societal, and strategic value of the stored content, it's not surprising that they've emerged as digital battlegrounds in our data-centric era. High profile cases like the Yahoo!, LinkedIn and Equifax data breaches stand as sombre reminders of the potential price of a security lapse.

2.3. Hackers: A Diverse Horizon

Not all hackers bear the mask of the adversary. The hacker milieu stretches far, encompassing a spectrum broader than the stereotypical disruptive force.

Ethical or 'white hat' hackers use their skills to anticipate and thwart security threats, working diligently to keep the cyberspace safe. They work either independently, reporting vulnerabilities to protect users, or in tandem with corporations, probing for cracks in their digital fortifications. These hackers play a crucial role in rebalancing this cyber-equilibrium, their intent aimed towards the protection of the online community.

On the other end, malicious or 'black hat' hackers adopt more sinister methods. Motivated by financial gains, ideological beliefs, or pure chaos, they exploit system vulnerabilities to perpetrate harm. They constantly devise intricate methods to bypass security, wreak havoc in databases, and leave trails of digital destruction in their wake.

Between the 'white hats' and 'black hats', other factions exist as well. 'Grey hat' hackers straddle moral boundaries; they do not cause harm but may operate without consent, detecting system weaknesses to bring attention to them. State-sponsored hackers work under the aegis of governments, commissioned to conduct cyber espionage and warfare. 'Hacktivists' use their skills to promote social or political agendas, attempting to bring about change through their actions.

This broad spectrum of hackers maintains a perpetual state of evolution in the realm of digital threats. The goalposts change; security responses must adapt in equal measure.

2.4. Cybersecurity: The Cycle of Defence

An effective cybersecurity protocol isn't a one-time setup; it's a dynamic, ongoing process. It's a tireless cycle of predicting, preventing, detecting, and responding to cyber threats. The defenders of the digital world, whether individual users or multi-billion dollar companies, must sustain their vigilance and adaptability. Firewalls, encryption, two-factor authentication, intrusion detection, and regular software updates are just some of the many shields in this digital armory.

Moreover, organisations must foster a culture of cybersecurity, teaching employees about safe online practices and the risk of phishing scams, ransomware, or malware. Consumers too must adopt precautionary measures to protect their data. Strong, unique passwords, safe browsing habits, educated software downloads, and keeping an eye out for suspicious activities can significantly reduce risk.

However, no system can ever be entirely impervious to cyber threats. As cybersecurity evolves, so too does the cunning and resourcefulness of hackers. Each side continually learning from the other, this invisible chess game never ends. Compromise is always a risk; hence, having robust incident response plans is paramount to mitigate any fallout swiftly and efficiently.

2.5. Looking Forward

In the coming chapters, we will delve further into the intricate makings of this virtual chess game. We will explore the multi-faceted world of hackers and the techniques they use, the challenges in protecting digital privacy, and the ways to cultivate proactive defenses. Whether you're an avid technology enthusiast or just starting on this digital journey, this comprehensive overview of the realm of hackers and cybersecurity will provide you with insights from both sides of the battlefield.

So, join us as we thread through the labyrinth, bridging gaps between the technical, the practical, and the raw human experiences at the heart of this digital battlefield. The game is on, and every player must understand the stakes. Our digital privacy hangs in the balance, and knowing is, indeed, half the battle. Remember, we are all participants in this digital war; it's time we understood what we're fighting for.

Chapter 3. The Anatomy of a Hack: Shedding Light on Dark Activities

In the vast universe of the internet, the act of hacking often takes the center stage of digitally dark activities. Let's begin by understanding the meaning of this term. Hacking, in its most rudimentary form, involves manipulating the normal functioning of a computer system or a network. While many associate this term with malicious intent, it's worth noting that not all hackers harbor harmful intentions.

It is clear that hacking, whether ethical or not, is an activity that requires an exceptional understanding of technology, combined with a unique ability to spot unnoticed vulnerabilities. A deeper glimpse into this often cladded world demands a comprehensive grasp of the anatomy of a hack. Let's explore this in more detail.

3.1. The Hacker's Mindset

Understanding the hacker's mindset is the starting point when peeling back the layers of a cyber attack. Just as a white hat (ethical) hacker, the black hat (malicious) hacker starts with one basic question: "How can I exploit this system?" They diligently search for vulnerabilities, sniffing out the weak points in a system that could provide them with an entry point.

3.2. The Discovery Phase

Once they choose a target, hackers usually spend a considerable amount of time in this initial phase. They research their potential victim, gathering as much information as possible. This includes understanding the hardware, software, network configurations, and any other data that could help them discern a flaw. They use various tools and methods for this, including passive information gathering, where they collect data without interacting with the target directly.

3.3. Scanning and Enumeration

After gaining sufficient background knowledge, hackers begin scanning the target system or network. Tools like port scanners help uncover open ports, services running on those ports, and the types of devices connected to the network. In the enumeration phase, they extract more in-depth details about the systems and networks, such as user names and group information, system roles, details about shared resources and network trusts.

3.4. Vulnerability Assessment

Following the enumeration, hackers now have a detailed understanding of the system or network. They draw on this to hunt for vulnerabilities or design flaws they can exploit. For publicly known vulnerabilities, they may even find an "exploit," code written by someone else that they can use to take advantage of these weaknesses.

3.5. Gaining Access

This is the crucial turning point, where hackers utilize discovered intelligence and vulnerabilities to breach the target. They may execute an exploit, engage in session hijacking or password cracking, inject malicious scripts, or perform any other method they find viable.

3.6. Maintaining Access

Once they achieve their unauthorized access, hackers typically strive to retain their foothold for future exploitation. They have multiple routes to do so, such as installing backdoors or rootkits, creating additional user accounts, or even modifying system logs to camouflage their activity.

3.7. Clearing Tracks

To evade detection, hackers exercise due caution to eliminate evidence of their intrusion. They meticulously clear system logs, command histories, and any other footprints that may disclose their presence.

3.8. The Aftermath

Finally, the hacker's mission concludes either by achieving what they set out to do, such as stealing information, disrupting services, or merely showcasing their skill, or by being discovered and terminated by the system's cybersecurity measures.

The understanding of a hack's structure and the steps involved is instrumental not only for those seeking to protect critical systems, but it also provides invaluable insight for individuals endeavoring to comprehend digital societal functioning. As we stride toward an increasingly interconnected era where technology promises to become even more embedded in our lives, understanding the underpinnings of these dark activities will be increasingly crucial.

In the following sections, we delve deeper into defensive strategies that can thwart such hacking efforts. We will discuss how you can arm yourself with knowledge and tactical skills, helping you navigate this digital battlefield that ceaselessly endeavors to compromise our digital privacy.

Chapter 4. Cybersecurity Basics: Building your Digital Armory

In the realm of cybersecurity, the first line of defense is knowledge: understanding the threats, recognizing the weaknesses, and gearing up with robust protections. This comprehensive overview of the fundamental concepts in cybersecurity will not only empower you with this knowledge but also guide you in fortifying your digital armory.

4.1. Understanding the Threat Landscape

The internet is vast, and not all its denizens have benign intentions. Cyber threats can come from anywhere, at any time. To effectively combat these, one must first comprehend the various forms they can take:

- *Malware:* Malware, or malicious software, comprises various forms including viruses, Trojans, and ransomware. They can wreak havoc on a system by corrupting files, stealing data, or even taking control of your entire machine.

- *Phishing:* This is a deceptive technique wherein an attacker attempts to trick you into sharing sensitive information like passwords or credit card numbers by impersonating a reliable entity, such as your bank or a trusted website.

- *Man-in-the-middle (MitM) Attacks:* Here, the attacker secretly intercepts and possibly alters the communication between two parties who believe they are directly communicating with each other.

- *Denial-of-service (DoS) and Distributed Denial-of-Service (DDoS) Attacks:* These attacks aim to overwhelm a system, network, or service with excessive traffic or requests, rendering it unavailable to its intended users.

4.2. The Weakest Link – Understanding Vulnerabilities

A chain is only as strong as its weakest link—the same holds true for your digital armor. Identifying and addressing vulnerabilities are crucial to keeping your armory impenetrable:

- *Software Vulnerabilities:* Bugs in the software can create 'backdoors' that hackers can exploit to infiltrate your system. Regularly updating your software helps patch these vulnerabilities.

- *Human Error:* Often, the most significant security lapses arise from human error—whether it's clicking on an unsafe link, using weak passwords, or accidentally disclosing confidential information.

- *Network Vulnerabilities:* Unsecured networks can provide a convenient access point for attackers—consider the case of unsecured Wi-Fi, where your communications can be intercepted without proper protection.

4.3. Building a Secure Digital Armory

Understanding the threats and weaknesses is the first step. The next is actively working to combat them. Let's look at some fundamental protective measures:

- *Antivirus and Antimalware Software:* This should be your

standard armor, serving as the primary line of defense against malicious software.

- *Firewall:* Acting as a digital gatekeeper, firewalls scrutinize incoming and outgoing traffic based on predefined rules, stopping potential threats at your network's edge.

- *Virtual Private Network (VPN):* A VPN serves as a secure tunnel for your online communications, shielding you from prying eyes and ensuring confidentiality.

- *Two-Factor Authentication (2FA):* An additional layer of security, 2FA ensures that even if your password is compromised, an attacker cannot gain access without the second verification factor, typically your smartphone.

4.4. Personal Security Best Practices

Software can only take you so far; responsible behavior can significantly boost your shield:

- *Strong Passwords:* Use passwords that are long, complex, and unique for each of your accounts. A password manager can keep track of these securely.

- *Phishing Awareness:* It's vital to scrutinize emails or messages that seem suspicious—especially those asking for personal information. When in doubt, contact the company directly using their official contact information.

- *Regular Software Updates:* These often include patches for security vulnerabilities. Install updates to all your software, including your operating system, applications and antivirus software, as soon as they become available.

- *Backup Regularly:* Having an up-to-date backup means that even if an attacker encrypts your files with ransomware, you can simply restore them from your backup.

In our struggle to safeguard our digital environment, armed with knowledge, we become the sentinels of our own cybersecurity. The more we familiarize ourselves with the risks and their countermeasures, the stronger our defenses grow. Understanding the essential cybersecurity basics equips us with the tools needed to navigate the digital world confidently and competently, making us less attractive targets for those lurking in the shadows of the world wide web.

Chapter 5. Privacy Breaches: The Stories that Shook the Web

In the past decade, the proliferation of digital technologies and ubiquitous internet connectivity have transformed how we live, work, and communicate. While the benefits are numerous, the rising tide of personal data exchange has also fueled an alarming growth in the number of privacy breaches. As we explore several of these incidents, it's key to remember these stories expose not only the vulnerabilities inherent in the digital revolution, but also underscore the importance of nurturing an informed ethos of digital privacy.

5.1. The Yahoo Data Breach: A Staggering Scale

The story of the Yahoo data breach begins in 2013, when hackers, suspected to be state-sponsored actors, hacked into Yahoo's network. They made away with personal information belonging to some 3 billion users, a staggering figure that represented every single Yahoo account at the time and making it the largest data breach in history.

What's even more alarming about this breach is that Yahoo didn't disclose it until 2016. Upon the announcement, the tech giant reported that data such as names, email addresses, dates of birth, hashed passwords, phone numbers, and, in some cases, encrypted or unencrypted security questions and answers were compromised.

This breach underscored the danger that not just individual users but the internet as a whole faces. Given that many users employ the same passwords and security questions across numerous platforms, one successful breach can potentially open the door to multiple violations of a user's digital privacy across the internet.

5.2. The Facebook-Cambridge Analytica Scandal: Wielded Data as Weapon

Another landmark case in the history of digital privacy breach is the Facebook-Cambridge Analytica scandal. The event unfolded in 2018 when it was revealed that Cambridge Analytica, a UK-based political consulting firm, had illegitimately accessed the data of 87 million Facebook users.

This data was weaponized to target voters with personalized political ads during the 2016 U.S Presidential election. Facebook's model of data collection and handling procedures allowed this immense breach of trust and privacy to occur, fuelling global uproar. The scandal highlighted that it wasn't just criminals and unknown parties users needed to worry about, but also the very platforms holding their data.

5.3. The Equifax Breach: A Blow to Financial Security

In 2017, Equifax, one of the largest credit reporting agencies in the world, announced a data breach that exposed the personal information of 147.9 million consumers. The breach lasted from mid-May through July, and the hackers accessed people's names, Social Security numbers, birth dates, addresses, and in some instances, driver's license numbers.

This was an alarming breach given the sensitivity of information that credit reporting agencies hold. The repercussions were wide-ranging with the potential for identity theft and financial havoc. The Equifax breach served as a stark reminder that organizations with highly sensitive information need to prioritize cybersecurity to protect the sanctity of personal data they handle.

5.4. The Twitter Bitcoin Scam: A Question of Trust

In the annals of recent digital privacy breach stories, the Twitter Bitcoin scam of 2020 stands out. This attack resulted in some of the most prominent accounts on Twitter, including those of Barack Obama, Jeff Bezos, and Elon Musk, among others, tweeting out requests for Bitcoin donations due to COVID-19.

A significant blow to Twitter's security infrastructure, this instance shows how privacy breaches can also lead to large-scale disinformation campaigns, undermining public trust in high-profile personalities and the platforms they use.

5.5. The SolarWinds Hack: A Stealthy and Systemic Breach

To conclude, we spotlight the SolarWinds hack—the massive, sophisticated digital intrusion that took place in 2020. Suspected state-sponsored hackers manipulated software developed by the Texas-based company SolarWinds, used by several U.S. government agencies and Fortune 500 companies, creating a backdoor to infiltrate their systems.

The breach was stealthy and systemic, lasting several months before detection, making it one of the most concerning episodes of cybersecurity failures. It underlined the potential national security risks and business risks associated with digital privacy breaches, prompting a call for better cybersecurity measures at all levels.

Through these tales of digital intrusions, we understand how breaches can impact individuals and societies. The lessons drawn from these landmark privacy breaches remain crucial in the scheme of the global digital framework, reinforcing the continuous need for vigilance, stronger cyber defenses, and resilient digital privacy norms.

Chapter 6. Entering the Mind of a Hacker: The Who, Why and How

Before diving into the inner workings of the hacker narrative, it's crucial to clear some preconceived notions. Often, society paints hackers with one broad, invariably nefarious brush. However, this monolithic picture is far from accurate. That's why we first need to understand the full spectrum of personalities within the hacking community.

6.1. Understanding Different Types of Hackers

In its simplest definition, a hacker is an individual who leverages their technical expertise to overcome a problem. In the context of cybersecurity, these quandaries typically revolve around infiltrating secured systems and networks. But not for the same purpose, nor with the same intent. Delving into this digital realm, you'll find three chief personas: white-hat, black-hat, and the nuanced grey-hat hackers.

'White-hat' hackers are the digital world's unsung heroes. They employ their profound technical understanding for the greater good, detecting system vulnerabilities and patching them before malevolent forces can exploit them. They often work hand-in-hand with governments, corporates, and organizations to fortify digital defenses, effectively serving as guardians of the virtual realm.

In contrast, 'black-hat' hackers are the harbingers of the digital apocalypse, the vandalizing graffiti artists of our interconnected world. Governed by motives far from altruistic, they exploit technological vulnerabilities for personal gain, propagation of chaos, or ideological struggle. They are the catalysts for fraud, data breaches, and disruption of services.

Somewhere amidst this dichotomy, lie 'grey-hat' hackers. A grey suit in a world of black and white, they straddle moral and ethical boundaries. Grey-hat hackers spotlight vulnerabilities without prior authorization but generally have benign intentions – to inform the network owner before graver risks materialize.

Understanding these varied personas should be the first step towards appreciating the hacker mindset and, in turn, effectively counter their moves.

6.2. The Driving Forces: Why Hackers Hack

Next, let's dissect the undercurrents that advance hackers across the digital landscape. Among the most common motives, you'll find financial gain, ideological beliefs, curiosity, and the simple joy of outsmarting systems.

At the top of the list, financial gain is a strong motivator, especially for black-hat hackers. They can sell stolen data or even hold it for ransom, as exemplified by the recent rash of ransomware attacks. Corporate secrets, personal identification information, even credit card details – these are all valuable commodities in the less savory corners of the digital world.

Hacktivism – hacking fueled by political or social ideologies – is the clarion call for many hackers. They weaponize their skills to amplify their voice, incite social change, or destabilize perceived adversaries. In a world that's more polarized than ever, hacktivism is on the rise.

For some hackers, the thrust may originate from sheer curiosity – the appeal of conquering challenges, understanding complex systems, and even outwitting intelligent defenses becomes an irresistible attraction. For these hackers, the act itself can be a thrilling cerebral exercise.

6.3. The Tactics: How Hackers Operate

To face an adversary, one must understand their tactics. In the context of hacking, these include reconnaissance, scanning, gaining access and maintaining it, and covering tracks.

Reconnaissance is the initial stage where hackers gather information about their target. They identify potential vulnerabilities going through public data, social engineering, or simply observing regular operations.

After having identified potential weak spots, hackers conduct a thorough scanning. They employ various tools to discern open ports, services being run, and system vulnerabilities that they can exploit.

Once weaknesses are detected, hackers proceed to gain unauthorized access. By leveraging vulnerabilities or using methods like social engineering, they infiltrate the system. Post penetration, they often aim to maintain access for prolonged periods, enabling them to maximize their manipulation or theft of data.

Lastly, covering tracks involves hackers erasing any indication of their intrusion. Rogue users can remain unnoticed for extended periods by careful manipulation of system logs, false alert triggers, and other discreet activities that shed their detection.

6.4. Conclusion: Guarding Against The Invader

Despite their varying motivations and approaches, hackers are becoming increasingly innovative and audacious in their tactics. Therefore, understanding and anticipating their moves becomes crucial in the battle for cybersecurity.

Nonetheless, protection against these threats is possible. As an individual or as an organization, it starts with maintaining a sense of vigilance, staying updated with evolving cyber threats and trends, and promoting strong cybersecurity practices. As we journey deeper into the digital age, cybersecurity literacy becomes indispensable – our shield in this ongoing battle to protect digital privacy. There are no bystanders in this war; we are all participants, knowingly or unknowingly.

In the following chapters, we will continue to delve deep into each of these areas, expanding upon the intricacies of cybersecurity measures, providing further insights into hackers' ever-evolving tactics, and most importantly, sharing practical strategies to stay one step ahead in this invisible yet critically impactful war.

Chapter 7. Digital Surveillance: The Role of Governments and Corporates

In the grand tapestry of the digital world, monitoring has evolved as a tool of both defense and control for governments and corporations alike. This meticulous watch over digital activity, known as digital surveillance, has a profound influence on our lives.

7.1. The Surveillance State: Governments at the Helm

Broad electronic surveillance programs have been implemented by many governments - sometimes clandestinely, compelling us to question the boundaries between security and privacy. These surveillance programs have become perplexingly comprehensive, leveraging a multitude of techniques.

A critical instance is the United States' National Security Agency (NSA) and their controversial surveillance program, PRISM. Disclosed by Edward Snowden in 2013, PRISM purportedly engages in extensive, untargeted collection of Internet communications. PRISM and other such programs globally, exemplify the "collect it all" approach, extracting information from communications between people not suspected of any wrongdoing.

Another surveillance model is the "Great Firewall of China", a combination of legislative actions and technologies to regulate the internet domestically. It enables state censorship and surveillance, blocking access to certain foreign websites and slowing down cross-border internet traffic.

Yet, even without such overarching mechanisms, surveillance is filtering down to localized levels too. Many cities globally have embraced the "Smart City" concept, which uses data collection and analysis to improve municipal services. While benefits are undeniable, so is the fact that almost every move can be documented, highlighting the critical question: At what point does security eclipse privacy?

7.2. Corporations: The Custodians of our Digital Lives

On the flip side of the coin, we find corporations, who, due to the nature of their business, store unimaginable amounts of data. If governments codify, corporates commercialize. Corporations, from mega tech companies to small app developers, collect, analyze, and often, sell user data without overt disclosure thereby playing a crucial role in digital surveillance.

Prominent among them are the Big Tech companies like Google, Facebook, Amazon, and others, whose core business models depend on data. Google, for instance, tracks your location even if you disable the 'location history' setting, raising questions about user consent and control over personal data.

Moreover, the advent of the Internet of Things (IoT) has accelerated data collection. Devices like smart speakers, home security systems, and even household appliances now collect data. They come with privacy trade-offs, often overlooked by users embracing the convenience these devices offer. A significant part of this problem lies in the long, convoluted privacy policies and lack of adequate user-friendly data control settings.

7.3. Surveillance Capitalism: A New Normal?

In fact, these practices have ushered us into the era of "surveillance capitalism," a phrase coined by Shoshana Zuboff. It refers to capitalism that is driven by profit from surveillance - a lucrative business built around selling user-data. By commodifying personal data, corporations have crafted a business model where users are the product.

Especially concerning is that surveillance capitalism distinguishes itself from traditional capitalism, which offers a trade-off between consumers and goods. In surveillance capitalism, most users are entirely unaware that their data is being harvested and commercialized. These practices, veiled by vague statements about "improving user experience", have far-reaching implications for individual privacy.

Yet another increasing concern is "data brokers," firms that exist solely to collect, analyze, and sell user data. These entities operate largely in the shadows, contributing to the invisible nature of this vast surveillance network.

7.4. The Battle for Privacy

Facing this new reality, individuals, civil society organizations, and governments have begun to fight back. Technological innovations, legislation, and advocacy are converging in this battle for privacy.

On the political front, law-making has shifted considerably, especially with the introduction of the European Union's General Data Protection Regulation (GDPR). Its rigorous provisions for data protection signaled a watershed in privacy legislation globally, impacting corporations and governments alike. While the GDPR has inspired similar laws globally, the fight for digital privacy is far from over.

Simultaneously, tech companies are feeling the pressure to respect privacy. Apple, for instance, has focused extensively on making privacy a selling point for their products.

In conclusion, although digital surveillance is an integral part of the digital domain, its threats to privacy are increasingly recognized and fought against. This chapter has outlined the tools and strategies employed by governments and corporates and the increasingly organized opposition they face. It has shown that digital surveillance is not an immutable reality. With legislation, technology, and a vigilant citizenry, the promise of a digitally private world might yet be within our grasp. The next section explores the world of hackers and activists who, in different capacities, feature prominently in this battle.

Chapter 8. Emerging Trends: AI and Quantum Computing in Cybersecurity

In the shadowy depths of the digital world, two technological forces - Artificial Intelligence (AI) and Quantum Computing – are dramatically reshaping the cybersecurity landscape. They make for powerful allies but can also potentially be weaponized into formidable threats. A nuanced understanding of these emerging trends will aid in preparing and defending against future cybersecurity challenges.

8.1. Artificial Intelligence (AI) in Cybersecurity

Artificial Intelligence is revolutionizing cybersecurity across the globe, bolstering defenses and paving the way for remarkable advancements. Equipped with machine learning (ML) algorithms, AI systems can sift through enormous data sets, identifying patterns that may signify a cyber threat faster than any human could.

Let us delve deeper into the pivotal role AI plays in cybersecurity – both as a friend and a potential adversary.

8.1.1. AI as a Cyber Defense Mechanic

As cyber threats continue to evolve, traditional security methodologies often fall short in detecting them. Here's where AI and ML make their grand entrance. They provide real-time threat detection by identifying irregular network patterns that human eyes might overlook. AI can dissect intricate cyber patterns, uncovering hidden threats – including malware and ransomware – thereby securing an organization's digital fortress.

Advanced AI systems conduct Predictive Analysis, preemptively pointing out potential future threats. Moreover, these systems never sleep, providing 24/7 monitoring to nip cyber-attacks in the bud, something a human-based workforce can never match in scope or speed.

Furthermore, AI-backed User and Entity Behavior Analysis (UEBA) are effective at pinpointing insider threats. By analyzing the baseline of standard user behavior – a shift in baseline attributes could indicate a potential security threat.

8.1.2. The Threat of AI-Powered Cyber Attacks

While AI is a potent protective shield, its potential for exploitation as a tool for cybercrime cannot be undermined. With adversarial AI, hackers can now automate phishing emails, making them more sophisticated and hard to identify. Adversarial AI can also manipulate ML models - a technique known as "poisoning" - to deceive security systems.

AI-empowered Deepfakes - manipulated multimedia content that fabricates reality, is a growing concern. Designed to trick users by replacing a person in an existing video with another's likeness, Deepfakes can wreak havoc if used maliciously, causing reputational and financial damage.

8.2. Quantum Computing in Cybersecurity

Moving to another powerful player in the technological arena - Quantum Computing. It boasts exponential computational prowess compared to classical computers, as Quantum Bits (Qubits) – contrary to classical bits – can be both 0 and 1 simultaneously, thanks to a quantum phenomena known as superposition.

This leap in computational capacity signals both promise and potential peril regarding cybersecurity.

8.2.1. Quantum Power: A New Defense Line

Quantum computing's potential to expedite tasks is monumental. Its immense processing speed and capacity to handle vast quantities of data quickly could revolutionize vulnerability detection systems, making them far more efficient compared to classical systems.

Furthermore, secure communication could become a reality with Quantum Encryption or Quantum Key Distribution (QKD). Thanks to Heisenberg's Uncertainty Principle, any attempt to intercept a quantum-encrypted communication would disturb the quantum state and alert the communication parties, making eavesdropping impossible.

8.2.2. Quantum Computing Threats

Quantum computing's immense power, in the wrong hands, poses significant security problems. Its ability to perform quick complex computations could easily break traditional encryption methods, including RSA and ECC - the primary encryption methods for secure online communication today.

With Shor's algorithm, a powerful quantum computing algorithm, even a well-equipped system can be compromised relatively quickly, leaving the world's digital doors wide open.

8.3. Preparing for the Quantum Age

With the dawn of quantum computing, drastic changes in security measures need to be implemented. Post-Quantum Cryptography (PQC) or Quantum-Resistant Cryptography is coming to the fore as experts worldwide gear to prepare for a new challenge.

While quantum supremacy is still years away, proactive steps are necessary to ensure we're prepared for the quantum leap. Encryption models able to withstand quantum attacks are under development while rigorous testing is undertaken to ensure they're fit for purpose. Prominent algorithms include Lattice-based, Hash-based, Code-based, and Supersingular Isogeny-based cryptography.

The emergence of these technologies – AI and Quantum Computing – signifies a new epoch in cybersecurity. While they are still evolving, their transformative effects on the world of cybersecurity are not to be underestimated. Therefore, ongoing research, awareness, and preparedness for these emerging trends remain key to ensuring a secure digital world.

Chapter 9. Countermeasures: Tactics to Protect Personal Online Data

The rise of the Internet age and interconnection of digital devices has made our personal data more vulnerable than ever. As the threats increase, so too do the countermeasures designed to protect our personal online data. These are multifaceted and span a range of differing approaches, timescales, and levels of technical expertise.

9.1. The First Line: Physical Security

Even in the digital age, physical security measures form a crucial part of protecting personal online data. The devices that store our information - computers, smartphones, external hard drives - should be adequately secured to deny unauthorized access.

Lock your devices whenever they are not in use. Many devices offer biometric security measures such as fingerprint or facial recognition, which can provide a significant enhancement to security. Encrypting your hard drive can protect the data it contains, even if the device itself is stolen.

If you're disposing of a device, remember it might still contain recoverable data. Simply deleting files doesn't guarantee they're gone forever. Use reliable tools to permanently shred unwanted files, or better yet, physically destroy the storage medium.

9.2. The Human Factor: Education and Awareness

One of the most potent threats to digital privacy is human error. The actions that people take, or fail to take, can often undermine even the most secure system. Educating yourself and others about cybersecurity risks and best practices is a fundamental countermeasure in this digital game of cat-and-mouse.

Phishing attacks - where attackers impersonate a trustworthy entity to trick you into disclosing sensitive data - have been a persistent vector of cyber threats. Understanding and identifying these forms of scams are critical. Online, if something appears too good to be true, it usually is.

9.3. Strong Authentication Practices

A strong security measure lies in strengthening access control to your personal data. Passwords must be robust and unique for each online service. Using a password manager can help manage this complexity and reduce the temptation to reuse passwords.

Two-factor authentication (2FA) and multi-factor authentication (MFA) are measures that can significantly enhance the security of your accounts. 2FA and MFA require you to authenticate your identity with two or more separate components, thereby making unauthorized access exceedingly difficult.

9.4. Regular Updates: Patching Vulnerabilities

No software is perfect; it contains vulnerabilities waiting to be discovered and exploited. Regularly updating your software -

operating systems, web browsers, antivirus software, apps - patches these vulnerabilities, making your digital environment a bit safer each time.

The importance of updates cannot be overstated. Many cyber threats prey on outdated software that has known and unpatched vulnerabilities. Even if updates can sometimes be disruptive and time-consuming, they provide essential protection for personal online data.

9.5. Firewalls and Antivirus Software

A robust defense also includes a good firewall and robust, up-to-date antivirus software. While not foolproof, these tools form a protective barrier between personal online data and potential threats.

A firewall monitors and regulates incoming and outgoing network traffic based on predetermined security rules, acting as a barrier between your device and the internet. Antivirus software, on the other hand, roams your device to locate and remove malicious programs.

9.6. Virtual Private Networks

A Virtual Private Network (VPN) can enhance protection by encrypting your online communications, making it harder for eavesdroppers to intercept them. By connecting to the internet via a VPN server, you mask your IP address and can browse more privately.

9.7. Data Backup

Backups represent a significant countermeasure against the threat of data loss stemming from a cyber attack. Regularly backing up your data ensures that, if the worst comes to pass, you can restore your system's operations more swiftly.

Backups should be periodic and automatic to ensure current data is protected. Remember the 3-2-1 backup rule: have at least three different copies of your data, store the copies on two different media, and keep one backup copy offsite.

9.8. Secure Internet Browsing

It's essential to be cautious while navigating the web to ensure your online activities don't expose you to unnecessary risk. Avoiding suspicious websites, using secure HTTP, clearing cookies, and limiting personal information online can limit your exposure to cyber threats.

9.9. Personal Responsibility

Ultimately, the security of personal online data relies on individual users taking ownership of their digital safety. Privacy settings should be evaluated and adjusted where necessary. Personal identifying information and sensitive transactions should be treated with maximum care and skepticism to maintain security.

In conclusion, protecting personal online data in the interconnected digital landscape is a multifaceted challenge. Still, one that can be actively managed and mitigated with the application of a range of countermeasures. By taking an active role in our own cybersecurity, we can help to dictate the narrative in this battle for digital privacy.

Chapter 10. The Future of Cybersecurity: Predictions and Prescriptions

As we look towards an increasingly interconnected future, the need to anticipate and adapt to emerging cybersecurity risks becomes an inescapable necessity. Technology's relentless evolution necessitates us to take a prospective glance at how cybersecurity may morph and change in the coming years. Here is an analysis of predicted trends, impending challenges, and necessary countermeasures that will shape the future of cybersecurity.

10.1. Changing Threat Landscape

The security threats we anticipate for the future will be an extension of what we face today. Ransomware has become a dominant form of cyber threat today. More often than not, a hacker will inject malicious software into a user's system, lock them out of their data, and demand a ransom payment to restore access. In the future, we may witness even more sophisticated ransomware attacks. Furthermore, cybercriminals could craft advanced artificial intelligence (AI) tools to implement these attacks at an alarming rate, exceeding human defenders' capabilities.

The Internet of Things (IoT) will also intensely expand the threat landscape. As we become more reliant on IoT devices in every walk of life, from smart homes to connected cars, we multiply the potential points of intrusion for hackers. The blurring of personal and professional boundary in an increasingly remote work culture adds to this increased vulnerability.

It is also cogent to note the threat of deepfakes looming on the horizon. Deepfakes use AI technology to create hyper-realistic but false images, audio, and videos to deceive and manipulate. Such methods of attacks have a high potential to cause disastrous consequences.

10.2. Evolving Cyber Defense Strategies

While the threat landscape evolves, so do the defense strategies to counter these attacks. The prophylactic measures and processes that we use today will have to adapt and innovate to match the pace of advancing threats.

We foresee AI assuming greater prominence in cybersecurity defenses. Machine Learning (ML) can predict patterns in behaviors that deviate from the norm, allowing it to identify anomalies and potential threats quickly and efficiently. It can process vast quantities of data, learning and improving over time. Deep Learning, a subset of ML, looks at minute patterns within subsets of data. The nuanced understanding offered by deep learning can aid in detecting refined, sophisticated attacks.

There's also significant potential in using quantum computing for defense strategies. While it could give hackers uncanny capabilities, it could also equip cybersecurity professionals with similar applications. Quantum encryption of data could offer robust security mechanisms and innovative ways to detect eavesdropping.

Furthermore, we anticipate a gradual shift from reactive to proactive cybersecurity strategies, known as cyber resiliency. This approach focuses on preparing systems to withstand and remain operational during an attack, ensuring that services will continue even under adverse conditions.

10.3. Regulatory Challenges and Policy Making

Regulation and policy-making will play significant roles in the future of cybersecurity. As online privacy concerns escalate, it is evident that legislative developments need sufficient pace and protection measures. Governments worldwide have started acknowledging the pivotal role of privacy and data protection laws in protecting their citizens.

However, the dilemma faced with this regulation will be ensuring stringent data protection without hindering technological innovation. Another crucial aspect will be international cooperation because cyber threats often transgress national boundaries. Harmonizing international regulations and formulating global cybersecurity standards can help resolve this.

10.4. The Human Element

Technology and regulation are only part of the solution. The human element is indispensable in dictating the success or failure of any cybersecurity strategy. The future of cybersecurity will entail a significant emphasis on galvanizing collective cybersecurity consciousness. A thriving security culture at all organizational levels is imperative - one that fosters cyber hygiene, nurtures awareness and encourages individuals to report suspicious activities.

Future societies will invest heavily in cybersecurity education and training. We anticipate a rise in cybersecurity as a career, and foresee an urgent need to bridge the current talent gap.

10.5. In Conclusion

The future landscape of cybersecurity, while replete with challenges, is not entirely dismal. Forward-thinking insights and strategic foresight can prepare us for the impending realities.

Modifying our cyber defense strategies, implementing strict yet flexible regulations, and empowering the human element are imperatives. Although uncertainty will always exist in cybersecurity predictions, the "prescriptions" discussed herein provide us with a roadmap.

As threats grow, we may weave these discussions into our risk awareness narrative. This awareness will bolster our resilience, enabling us to exploit the tremendous potential the digital future holds, conscientiously and securely. The ultimate aim should be to create a cyber environment that identifies potential threats, mitigates risks, and learns from every security incident, moving us closer to a more robust and resilient cyber ecosystem.

Chapter 11. Conclusion: Empowering Yourself in the Digital Age

In this era of rapidly evolving technology, the internet has become indispensable. It's a magnificent tool that has revolutionized communication and redefined society. It's a global library of information, a platform for businesses, and a meeting point for millions. However, while we enjoy the benefits of this interconnected digital landscape, we must also brace ourselves for the inevitable risks – cyber threats.

Cyber threats, intrusions, and security breaches have become part of our daily lives. Yet, it's no longer merely an issue of security; it's an issue of survival. In this dangerous landscape, the only way to defend ourselves and safeguard our digital privacy is to be well-informed, vigilant, and proactive.

11.1. Understanding the Threat Landscape

In the world of cybersecurity, there's no dearth of enemies. Be it state-sponsored hackers, cybercriminals, or even malicious insiders, the threat landscape is expansive and ever-changing. Understanding these potential threats – and recognizing that they exist – is the first step in defending ourselves.

State-sponsored hackers represent nations indulging in cyber espionage, seeking to steal sensitive data to gain a strategic edge. Despite their impressive resources, they are not invincible. Countries worldwide are working on robust cybersecurity strategies to counter these threats.

On the other hand, cybercriminals aim for personal gain, often targeting individuals and businesses. They exploit weaknesses in our digital defenses and use sophisticated techniques, such as ransomware or phishing, to steal our data, money, or identities.

Malicious insiders, whether disgruntled employees or careless staff, represent another significant threat. Their in-depth knowledge of our systems and easy access to sensitive information can wreak havoc if left unchecked.

Understanding these threats empowers us to prepare for and identify any potential attacks on our digital privacy.

11.2. Importance of Proactive Defense

In the fight against cyber threats, a proactive stance is our strongest defense. Rather than waiting for an attack to occur, we must continually scan our networks for vulnerabilities and promptly patch them.

Implementing multi-factor authentication is another key step. This adds an extra layer of security to your online accounts and significantly reduces the risk of unauthorized access.

Backups are also crucial in maintaining digital privacy. Regular, encrypted backups to a secure offsite location can safeguard our data if our primary systems are compromised.

11.3. The Power of Knowledge

Being well-informed is crucial to protecting ourselves in the digital age. Knowledge, in this context, includes understanding complex cybersecurity concepts, identifying potential threats, and implementing state-of-the-art security practices.

There's a wealth of information available online, ranging from cybersecurity blogs and industry journals to online courses and webinars. Supporting constructive dialogue about cybersecurity and promoting a culture of continuous learning within organizations and homes helps enhance everyone's cyber hygiene.

Awareness of basic cybersecurity tenets—such as recognizing phishing emails, securing data, using strong passwords, and regularly updating software—is particularly essential.

11.4. The Role of Legislation and Policy

While individual efforts play a significant role in digital privacy, they are not enough. Governments worldwide need to enact comprehensive legislation and policies to protect their citizens and ensure a safe cyber environment.

There are no silver bullet solutions in cybersecurity and privacy legislation. Legislations must be flexible to adapt to the changing threat landscape. Governments must work with the private sector, academia, and civil society to craft comprehensive and effective laws.

Furthermore, international cooperation is key. Since cyber threats know no boundaries, nations must pool their resources and intelligence to counter them effectively.

11.5. Technology: The Double-Edge Sword

Technological innovations have always been a mixed blessing. On one hand, they empower us. On the other hand, they often result in new vulnerabilities.

As we look forward to advanced technologies such as artificial intelligence, the Internet of Things, and quantum computing, we must also be prepared for the fresh set of challenges they represent in the privacy and security landscape.

Harnessing the power of these emerging technologies for cybersecurity can be one of the best strategies. Leveraging machine learning algorithms for threat detection and automating security patch updates are examples of how these technologies can bolster our defense posture.

11.6. Conclusion: The Battle Continues

As we step further into the digital age, the battle to protect digital privacy continues. Remember, the power to protect ourselves largely rests in our hands. By understanding the threats, adopting best practices, remaining vigilant, and advocating for robust legislation, we can contribute significantly to this battle.

The importance of promoting a security-centric culture, both in our personal lives and in the wider society, cannot be understated. To survive and thrive in the digital age, we must recognize cybersecurity as an integral part of our digital citizenship. With empowerment, vigilance, and knowledge, we can ensure our precious digital privacy is well protected.